Prolance

www.prolancewriting.com
California, USA
©2020 Yousfa Janjua

ISBN: 978-1-7345760-0-9

My First Muslim Potty Book

Yousfa Janjua
illustrated by Golnar Servatian

PROLANCE

Dedicated to
my baby ninjas

This book, written in rhyme, serves as a gentle and fun introduction to potty training and Islamic toilet etiquette for little Muslims and Muslimahs. It aims to introduce and normalize "Muslim potty training," which includes *istinja*, to your child. *Istinja* is the act of cleaning oneself with water and then wiping oneself dry after using the bathroom. Muslims do this to keep themselves physically and spiritually clean and pure or in a state of *Tahara*. Toddlers will learn that their parents will do *istinja* for them until they are old enough to do so themselves. Reading and following along will mentally prepare toddlers to be happy and willing potty trainees, motivate them to try a new skill and teach them the basic Islamic technique to bathroom hygiene and etiquette. Also, the beautiful illustrations, by Golnar Servatian, portray diverse and relatable Muslim characters and experiences, to offer your child a feeling of representation and inclusivity; laying the foundation of a strong Muslim identity.

In general, there are many ways to begin potty training. In this author's opinion, starting on the adult toilet, like the character of this story, is easiest way to do *istinja* and easiest method to manage both inside and outside the home. However, remember that each child is different and will reach milestones at his or her own pace. Follow your child's developmental signs and cues of potty training readiness. The common signs are that he or she:
* has dry diapers in the morning
* can verbalize or show signs of being aware of when he/she has to go
* has the motor skills to pull their pants up and down
* has fewer wet diapers throughout the day

Please remember to be patient with your little one. Reward his or her successes and treat accidents with understanding and love. It is normal to start anywhere between 2 to 3.5 years of age but adding potty books at an earlier age will help ensure a smoother training.

Insha'Allah you and your toddler will find this book helpful and fun.
Happy Muslim Potty training!

You were once little; babbling and crawling.
Then you learned to talk and walk without
falling.

May you keep growing and learning; that is our prayer.

So bye-bye diapers! Hello big kid underwear!

You are a big kid now and so you should know,
Big kids use the potty, when they need to go.

When you're feeling full or pressure down below,
Time to get on the potty: move fast, not slow!

If you have an accident while you hurry,

We will clean it all up, love—don't you worry!

Enter with your left foot,
whether you walk or run,
To get to the potty and
get the job done.

Then pull down
your pants and big
kid underwear.

Ask for help if you
need it- that's why
we are there!

And sit down to make pee or sit down to make poo,

Because that's what big kids on the potty must do!

Poo and pee are *najis*, which means impure.

So get out every plop n' drop and always make sure...

To do istinja!

(It's kind of like being a germ fighting ninja!)

Muslims use water to wash their private parts.

Pay close attention this is how *istinja* starts:

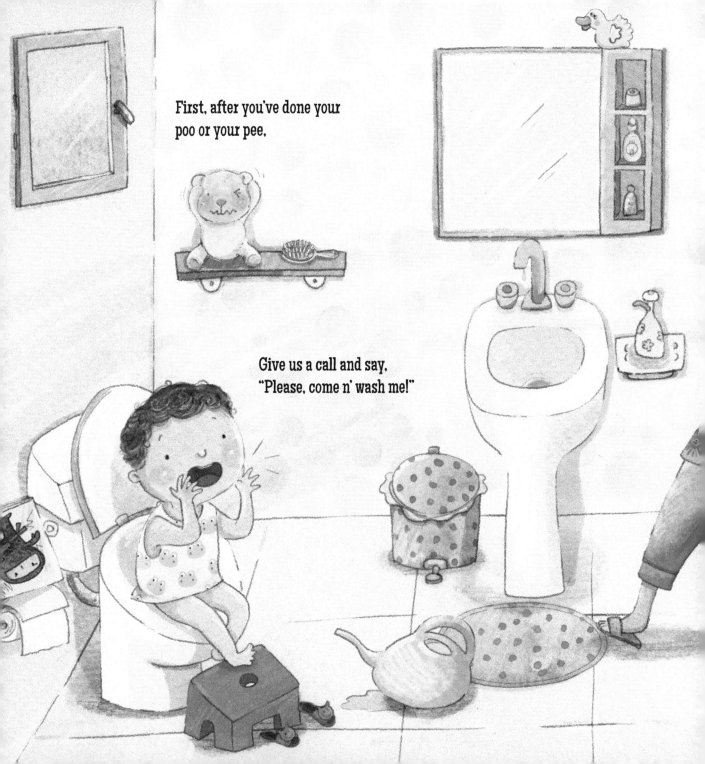

First, after you've done your poo or your pee,

Give us a call and say, "Please, come n' wash me!"

With water from a bidet, lota or pot,
We will clean you just like all Muslims
are taught.

The left hand washes while the right hand pours.
Once you are older this task will be yours.

Using toilet paper we'll wipe you dry.
You could wipe yourself if you wanted to try.

Istinja is over and clothes come back on.
We flush the potty and the waste is all gone!

Head to the sink, take a
step on the stool,
Wash your hands; 20
seconds, that's the rule!

You're all clean little one!
Great job! What fun!
Exit with your right foot
and you're all done!

Now you're in a state of *Tahara* or purity,

As all Muslims must be when they reach maturity.

The Prophet, whom we send peace upon, Said, "Cleanliness is half of *Emaan*,"

Allah loves those who are pure and clean.
May you keep growing and learning your *Deen*,
And get potty trained with good Muslim hygiene!
Ameen!

Glossary

This is a general introduction to Islamic terms and etiquette for toddlers. I encourage all parents to build and explore these topics in greater detail outside the scope of this book with your child.

Allah
The One and Only God. The Arabic word for God.

Deen
The religion of Islam.

Emaan
Belief or faith in Islam.

Istinja
Is the act of washing your private parts with water with your left hand after pooing or peeing and drying yourself afterwards.

Maturity (Islamically)
The age your actions, good or bad, are recorded for Allah. This is around age 12 for many kids, but can be sooner or later.

Muslim
Someone who believes in One God and that Prophet Muhammad, peace be upon him, is His last and final messenger. A follower of Islam.

Najis
Something that God has revealed is dirty and unclean like poo or pee.

Tahara (after using potty)
Is being totally clean and pure in Islam. This means removing all waste from your body (every drop and plop), doing *istinja* and finally washing your hands. Muslims must always try to be in a state of *Tahara*. They need to be in a state of *Tahara* to do things like wudu to pray.

Quran & Hadith

Quran 9:108 Surah At-Tawbah:
"...Allah loves those who make themselves pure."

Quran 2:222 Surah Al-Baqarah:
"...Allah loves those who turn to him constantly and He loves those who keep themselves pure and clean."

The Prophet Muhammad, peace be upon him, said: "Cleanliness is half the faith (Emaan)." (Sahih Muslim)

The Prophet Muhammad, peace be upon him, taught us to eat, drink, start wudu and serve others with our right hand and to use the left hand to clean our private parts after using the bathroom. Muslims are always mindful of Allah in everything they do.

The Prophet Muhammad, peace be upon him, also taught us to sit down to use the toilet. This is important so that najis pee or poo doesn't spread everywhere.

Duas to Learn

When entering bathroom: Enter with your left foot and say;

اللّهُمَّ إِنِّي أَعُوذُ بِكَ مِنَ الْخُبُثِ وَالْخَبَائِثِ

(Bismillaah) allaahumma innee aaoodhu bika minal-khubuthi wal-khabaa'ith
O Allah, I seek refuge with you from all evil and evil-doers.

When leaving bathroom: Exit with your right foot and say;

غُفْرَانَكَ

Ghufraanaka
I ask You (Allah) for forgiveness.

Printed in the USA
CPSIA information can be obtained
at www.ICGtesting.com
LVHW061451210124
769470LV00014B/270